Boston Terriers

A Pet Guide for Boston Terrier

Boston Terrier General Info, Purchasing, Care, Cost, Keeping, Health, Supplies, Food, Breeding and More Included!

By Lolly Brown

Foreword

Before you welcome a pet into your live, the first thing that you need to do is research all you can about this particular pet. You will look at web sites, books, and magazines for all the information you can get. Aside from this, you will talk with your breeders, friends, dog clubs, and even your neighbors. You will gain as much as knowledge as you can so you will choose the right pet and the right breed for your family.

Boston Terriers are called the American Gentleman. This nickname would make the breed sound serious, noble, and reserved. However, Boston Terriers, are bred with low brow humor, together with their funny faces, and hilarious antics – you will never get bored if you have this breed!

In this book, we will give you a detailed guide on how to love and take care of your Boston Terrier. Aside from this, we will also make sure that this breed is right for you and your family, as well as the set-up of your family. We would also discuss the different needs and wants of this breed, to make sure you have enough budgets before taking this breed home.

We hope that this book will help you in deciding that you need to get a Boston Terrier now!

Table of Contents

Introduction

Of over 340 dog breeds around the world, the Boston Terrier surely stands out!

Also known as the American Gentleman, the Boston Terrier surely stands out to its name. It is a crossbred in the United States of America! Aside from this, this breed has been designated the State Dog of Massachusetts.

These dogs are intelligent, compact, lively, friendly, and well balanced. It appears like this breed is wearing a tuxedo through its striking dark coat with flashy white markings.

The Boston Terrier loves to interact with people and other pets, especially with other Bostons. It really loves kids especially if they are monitored and socialized properly.

Another great thing about this breed it is apartment friendly due to its size!

There are still a lot of things you need to know about the Boston Terrier, just like its housing requirement, food and nutrition, and even its health concerns.

You need to know that you need to take care of the dog, from the day that it comes to your life until the day that it dies. Your stay with your dog is not just about rainbows and butterflies, sometimes, things will go wrong – so you need to also be prepared.

This book will help you to know everything you need to know about the Boston Terrier. We will give you reasons why you need to get a Boston Terrier dog today!

We hope that by the end of this book, you will gain a lot of knowledge and appreciation of the breed and will truly love this breed as we love it. Enjoy reading!

Chapter One: Tracing the Boston Terrier's History

What picture pops into your mind when you think of a Boston Terrier? You would probably think a dog with an unmistakable pug nose with cute and pointy ears. It also has a unique tuxedo as a coat, or listening to its lovely wheezing and snorting that you will surely hear as it approaches you. Before you go out and get yourself your own Boston Terrier in your own home, you need to know the things that will make this dog tick. In this chapter, we will be discussing to you the wonderful history of the Boston Terrier. Aside from this, we will also give you quick facts about the breed, as well as personality pluses that make this breed truly stand out.

A Lover, Not a Fighter

Boston Terriers are popularly known as the American Gentleman, and it is for a good reason. This breed is affectionate, intelligent and classy dog that loves company and would do great as house companions.

With its loving and caring personality, you would not believe that the ancestors of this breed were originally bred to fight other dogs!

The Early Days

The Boston Terrier is the mix of the white English Terrier, who is now extinct, and the English Bulldog. One of the first dogs belonging to this breed was named Hooper's Judge, who was owned by Robert C. Hooper from Boston, Massachusetts. The bulldog-terrier blend was imported from Native England around 1870. Hooper's Judge was described to be a high-stationed, dark brindle dog with a lot of white markings. This dog looked more a Bulldog rather than its other mix.

In this time, the cross between the terriers and bulldogs that were used in Britain and the United States were used for blood sports such as pit dog-fighting and bull-baiting, however, this sports was later outlawed.

Many early breeders from the United States admired the dog's look, so they further refined and stabilized the look of this breed, further selecting smaller sizes, with large expressive eyes and has a likable personality. This mix is what we know the current Boston Terrier today.

A number of Boston Terrier's fanciers around the Boston Area formed the American Bull Terrier Club in 1889. This club exhibited dogs as Bull Terriers or Round Heads.

In 1891, another group of Boston Terrier breeders and fanciers formed the Boston Terrier Club of American, they renamed the breed to Boston Terrier. The group followed the origin of the breed. It took a number of years before the AKC was persuaded that Boston was a purebred that would produce great breed.

They were extremely popular in the early 1900s. It placed either the first or second on the list of registered breeds from the years 1905 to 1934 in the American Kennel Club.

By the 1920s, the breed has reached Europe while the 1950, it became one of the most popular breed in North America.

Boston Terriers were welcomed among socialites and fanciers alike. Every family wants to own a Terrier! Over the course of the century, they have gained a great position in the AKC's most popular dog; they consistently sit on among the top 20 popular dogs!

Right now, these dogs have made their way into different households, varying from small apartments to large farms and wherever possible! They have truly captured the hearts of a lot people around the world!

Personality Plus

If you ever come across Boston Terrier owners, you would surely hear nothing but praises for this breed, which is probably true because they are intelligent, loving, and ready for any activity that you would want to do!

Here are the other reasons why you should love and have a Boston Terrier:

They love kids

Most Boston Terrier loves to bond with kids. When kids are taught how to behave and love dogs, the dog and kids would become best friends so face! The dog would enjoy wrestling matches, playing dress up or even going out for a quick run! These little mutters would love to do anything with their children.

They adore adults

Boston Terriers get along with seniors, adults, and children alike. They can integrate well into any households.

Some Boston Terrier are even bred to become therapy dogs, some travel to nursing home to bring joy to old and aging patients.

They are low maintenance

Boston Terriers are easy to take care of. They have short coats that can be easily brushed and washed. They don't require a lot of exercise because they have low energy. Aside from this, they are very intelligent, great with house training, and even obedience training.

They are a healthy breed

Although they may have problems due to their short snout, Boston Terriers are healthy dog.

They can fit anywhere!

Boston Terrier is the perfect size for any type of houses, such as, town house, apartment, or even single-family home. They do not really require a large yard which makes them wonderful house pets.

They like other pets too.

Boston Terriers are an easy going breed. They love to share their homes and space with other cats, dogs, and even a caged hamster! Just make sure you introduce the other pets slowly, and they will get along easily.

Quick Facts

In this part, we will give you a quick rundown on the essential information about your pet the Great Dane. These information can serve as your 'cheat' sheet in the future.

Origin: United States

Pedigree: cross breed of the English Bulldog and the English Terrier (which is now extinct)

Breed Size: non-sporting group

Body Type and Appearance: smooth coated, short-headed, built compactly, short-tailed, but still well balanced.

Group: American Kennel Club

Height: Males are 17 inches tall and Females stand at 16 inches tall.

Weight: 15-25 lbs. for males while 10-20 lbs. for females

Coat Length: short and flat

Coat Texture: glossy

Color: brindle with white, black and white, seal with white

Temperament: friendly, lively, intelligent,

Strangers: friendly around strangers

Other Dogs: loves other dogs

Other Pets: gets along well with other pets

Training: easy to train

Exercise Needs: less than 20 to 40 minutes of exercise per day

Health Conditions: overall healthy but may come across several diseases or illnesses due to their brachycephalic (squashed face)

Lifespan: average 10-14 years

We have rounded up everything you need to know about our loving and beloved Boston Terrier. This is just the surface of the deep and wonderful world for this breed. We need to get along to other chapters to get to know more about this beloved creature.

Chapter Two: A Lifetime with the Boston Terrier

A happy and healthy Boston Terrier will surely greet anyone with a very big smile! However, you need to commit at least 15 years (or even more) is a long time and not should be taken lightly. Are you ready for this challenge?

Aside from this, are you prepared to take in an intelligent, energetic, and well-mannered dog into your own house? High spirited and loving, just like our Boston Terrier, needs a lot of understand and tolerance. This breed is highly intelligent and will develop a lot of interests and wants a lot of challenges to keep their minds and hearts occupied.

If you ever want to welcome a dog into your home, you should not only consider the breed but also your needs too. Your lifestyle and family set-up needs to match with the needs of the dog that you want to have.

In the pages to follow, you will discover a lot more responsibilities that you need when you are raising a Boston Terrier. Aside from this, we will also help you to license and register your loving Boston Terrier. This will help you and your family to commit to care for your chosen breed, the Boston Terriers.

Are You Compatible?

The Boston Terrier, the American Gentleman, will surely complement any household that it will go to. It is entertaining, kind, comical, and gentle, and will surely make you happy with its funny personality and antics.

This breed makes wonderful pets, especially for families with active and young members, or even a single person that plans to have a companion in the house.

A great thing about this pet is their love for children. Adult Boston Terrier are known to love any form of teasing and even roughhousing your child could give! Because of their well-mannered and gentle ways, this breed is idea for seniors who will not be able to exercise their pets daily.

If you believe you and your family can commit to give the dog what it needs to have, like a regular training time, understanding, patience, constant companionship, and giving lots of attention and love – this breed may be the best for you!

What Does My Terrier Need?

The Boston Terrier is curious yet very lively and very far from the antics of his ancestors. In order to have a happy Boston Terrier, you may need to provide the following to your dog:

SECURITY

Boston Terriers are not great guard dogs. They will rarely bark, unless they want to say something to you. It will welcome anyone with a playful wag and lick, and, it would go home with anyone – as long as the dog has given enough attention and treats. For this obvious reason, you need to provide a fence or keep the dog in an enclosed yard. And when you want to go to for a walk, you need to have the dog on a leash.

TRAINING

The Boston Terriers are very intelligent,which is why they are great students at basic training classes and even puppy academies! They would want to play with their classmates or even chase a butterfly, because they are easily distracted, but with great patience and persistence – it will surely pay off in no time.

INDOOR LOVING

Because your Boston Terrier has a short, flat nose and short coat, it would like to spend its time with you at the comfort of your own home. It would not like and can't tolerate changing and extreme weathers well. During summer time, you need to provide it with a cool, shady area for staying, while during winter, you may need to bundle it up before you go outside (or even stay inside).

A REGULAR SCHEDULE

When you welcome the dog into your house, you need to welcome it with loving arms. Each one of your family members should dedicate enough time to taking care and even nurturing the puppy or even an adult dog. You need to assign chores to each family member, and you need to come up with the same training technique. You need to remember that this dog is part of your family now.

I Want A Boston Terrier Because…

- sturdy and small, not a fragile lapdog.
- cute big puppy eyes
- a beautiful sleek yet easy to take care of coat
- polite with just around anyone – including other pets
- loves to chase balls as well as play games

I Don't Want A Boston Terrier Because…

- it will snort, wheeze, slobber, snuff, and even snore
- it will pass up a gas!
- very slow or even difficult to housebreak
- many health problems due to its facial deformities

The Real Costs

Having a dog in your life is not really cheap. However, you have some costs that will include dog food, supplies, bills, and cleaning supplies. But, have you ever calculated the total costs? In this portion, we will break down the cost into owning your Boston Terrier:

One-time and Monthly Expenses

For dogs, you have one-time expenses as well as monthly expenses when you bring home your Boston Terrier.

- **One Time Cost: Dog Ownership**
  - An average owner would spend around $655 for small purebred dogs. You can expect to pay $650 and up if you want to purchase a Boston Terrier, but still depends on where you live.

  - Adopting a Boston Terrier from a rescue or shelter would cost less. A purebred adult dog could value at $300 or even less, which even includes neuter or spaying and even vaccinations.

  - You also need to have your dog neutered and spayed. The cost for this surgery is around $160.

  - You also need to ready around $350 on training fees and supplies, and reports.

  - You also need to spend around $350 for non - consumable pet products such as a crate, bowls, and leash.

- **Ongoing Expenses**
  - You need to prepare a budget for expenses and consumable items, such as leashes, food, medication, and treats.

  - The average cost of vet visits, grooming, treats, food, travel, boarding, and toys is around $2489 per year. You may also need to prepare money for training and dog events. However, the cost will depend on where you live.

Unexpected Costs

An expense that you can't really plan is for an emergency. An emergency vet visit will cost around $631. However, some might even spend around $594.

If your dog requires emergency care, you need to spend big bucks to keep your dog healthy. However, you can plan your dog care through a health insurance. You may even need to spend around $300 to $400 a year, but, this will save you thousands of dollars when your dogs need emergency and critical care.

Consult your breeder, vet, or even the internet for pet health insurance companies. You can also ask your friends or members of the Boston Terrier Club for their referrals.

Like any other insurance, you need to pay a premium every month. This will result to a policy that covers prescription flea prevention, vaccinations, accidents, surgeries, annual exams, heartworm protection, hospitalization, radiology, and even cancer treatments. Your insurance will pay a percentage of the total medical costs.

The only difference between the pet and human insurance is that, you need to pay the bill immediately, prepare a claim form, and, then, get reimbursed for the total medical costs. This will allow you to take your pet to any licensed vet without worrying about the cost. However, if you do not want to get pet insurance, you need to prepare several hundred dollars for emergencies.

License and Registration!

In many countries, you really need to license and register your Boston Terrier. You need to apply and obtain dog license from your local animal control after you have brought the puppy or dog at home.

You also need to register your dog to either a national or international dog registries. The process will begin of the breeder, because she or he needs to register the dog's litter. When you take ownership of the dog or puppy, the breeder will pass on the dog registration application to you, which you need to accomplish and mail to the organization needed. You can either do this before or after you have brought the Boston Terrier at home, but this must be done before your dog reaches the age of one.

Please Make Me Legal!

Countries or states have certain laws for licensing your dog, but this depends well on where you live. This dog license will earn you a right to legally own the dog. The agency will issue you an identification number and a dog tag that will bear the number of your Boston, which must be worn by the dog at all times.

There are certain laws that will protect your dog and other animals against rabies, which can possibly threaten their lives. When you license your Boston Terrier, it will ensured that your dog will be returned to you once it wanders off away from home and is picked up by animal control.

The money that you will pay for licenses will be used for thousands of animals for their homes, aside from this, some money will be used for finding homes to other dogs, and some money will be put for spaying and neutering programs.

If you want to apply for a dog license, contact your local animal control agency immediately. They will give you a form that needs your name, address, phone number, as well as your pet's vital information. The agency will even require you to submit the latest copy of the dog's rabies vaccination and sterilization records.

When your licensing is approved, you will get a licensing tag that has a unique number that you will attach to the dog's collar and you need to make sure that you wear this at all times.

The fees for license and registration will depend on the area, however, unaltered animals would cost more that neutered or spayed animals. Animal agencies will also you renewal forms yearly.

Be One with AKC and UKC

The United Kennel Club (UKC) and the American Kennel Club (AKC) are two well-known dog registries in the world. Dog registries needs specific requirement for eligibility. If you want your dog registered, the parents and the litter must be also registered by both the owner and the breeder. You also need to check the clubs for specific registries. Here are some benefits of registering your Boston Terrier:

- Getting a certificate of registry
- Having a permanent record of the dog in the UKC or AKC registry.
- Having access to several benefits. Such as free pet healthcare trial, certificate of free veterinary visit,

puppy handbook, a pass to participate in competitive AKC-approved events.

These are just some of the reasons why you need to register and license your dog immediately. Make the decision now and register your pet in the nearest animal control agency

Chapter Three: The Battle of the Sexes

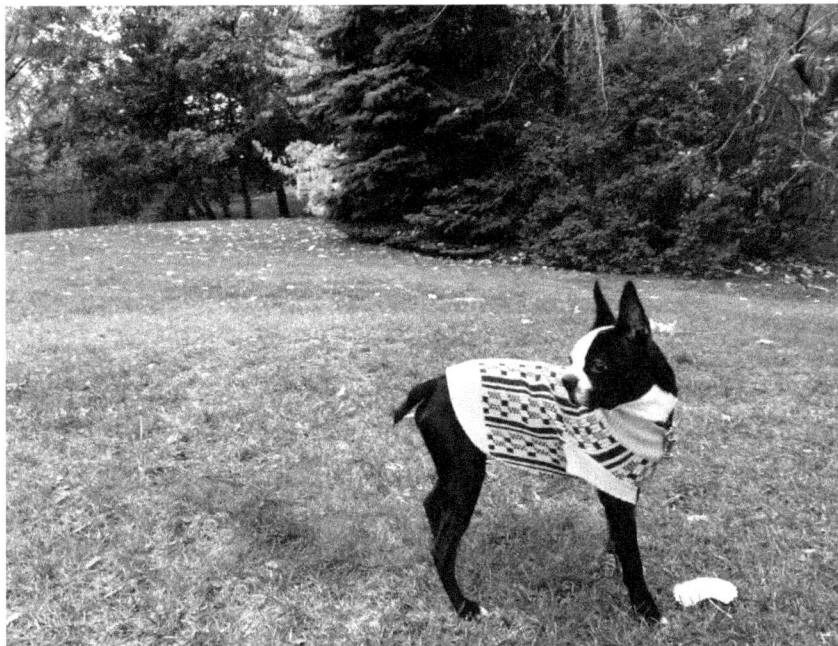

It is common that you follow what you feel when you select a new dog. You can easily fall in love with any adorable puppy that you can see, you may even take the dog home easily! However, you are not really prepared or do not have enough time to take care and share your life with a dog.

You will have ease of success for adoption if you already know what breed, age, and gender will suit you and your family the best. With your chosen breed, Boston Terrier, it is now time to decide whether you will get a male or female dog, and whether you will get adult or puppy.

In this chapter, we will discuss the personalities of the female and male Boston Terrier. We will also compare the qualities of the adult and puppy. You will be educated about these things then you will have a great decision about what kind of Boston Terrier is right for you.

If you have decided the gender and gender of your Boston Terrier, you need to find one. We will also discuss the different sources for finding a dog, which includes the rescues, breeders, newspaper advertisements, and even pet stores.

The Battle of the Sexes

Just like humans, both the male and female Boston Terriers have distinct characteristics that make them very unique. You will see these differences easily when your dog is not yet neutered or spayed.

Males are very devoted and loyal companions, but they will make their own territories. Females, on the other hand, come into heat twice a year, so you need to guard them from male dogs. If you want to spay or neuter your Boston Terrier, many of these gender characteristics will change, but the personality will not.

Boston Terrier males are larger than females. Aside from this, these two genders look the same. It is your personal reason which gender you want to choose.

Mighty Males

Male Boston Terriers will make devoted and loving companions. They are the true American gentlemen, but are also entertaining and playful. They have a constant mood, but could be raucous and rowdy, depending on the dog's individual personality.

Males would naturally find females in heat, they are prone to running off and searching for someone to mate. Adolescent males will also challenge you through disobeying your commands, especially if there is female dog in the area. You may need to have extra patience during training and obedience sessions.

Male dogs who have not been neutered will lift their legs to mark their territory, to let the other dogs know that the yard and home are his turf. Dogs will do this even if they are housetrained or not, make sure you have some odor-busting products in your cleaning shelf.

Neutered males do not have this problem, aside from this, they will not roam, mark their territories, be aggressive, and rebel against you. Unless you want to breed your pet or show off your dog, you should have your dog neutered.

Loving Females

Female Boston Terriers are naturally loyal and sweet companions. They have mother-like instincts that will influence her human family too.

Unlike the male counterpart, un - spayed female Boston Terrier will be temperamental and moody, especially during its heat seasons (which will be twice a year). When this season comes, make sure you isolate the female from the male, because she will be ready to mate to whoever she looks at. Other than this, you also need to clean the blood during the time. If you plan to spay your female Boston Terrier, your dog will not be really bossy, she will have emotional consistency.

Puppy or Adult: What Shall I choose?

Puppies are cute and cuddly creatures. Your heart will literally melt when your puppy's big round eyes see through you. The puppy needs to be taken care of in every way possible. You need to show it how to act, where to sleep, and how to play and when to play. You will be personally responsible to mold her behavior and personality.

On the other hand, the adult dog will be a delight. It has already passed the awkward puppy stage and will become independent and very manageable. It well depends on its training skill and history, but you will not spend as much time in training and obedience classes, and will be ready to be your constant companion.

Planning to get a puppy or adult dog will be a difficult task. Before you make this decision, you need to ask yourself:

- Can you allot time for training and raising a puppy?

    If you have time flexibility or even work at home, bringing a puppy at home is right for you! However, if you do not have time, an adult dog that has been fully housetrained, and that is relatively independent.

- Is your lifestyle suitable to raise a dog?

    If you are a home buddy, raising a puppy would be right for you. However, if you enjoy going out with friends and family, an adult dog is better for you and your lifestyle.

- Would you want to breed your dog?

    If you want to breed your dog right now, you need to find a good breeder who is willing to give you a young-adult female dog that is nearing her adult temperament and conformation.

- Do you really want to see your puppy grow up?

  If you want to watch your dog grow up, you can choose a puppy. An adult dog, on the other hand, already has its own personality and may have some behavioral issues from its previous owner or place where you got it.

- Do you have children at home?

  Young children may not be ready for raising a puppy, older children could help you with chores in raising up a puppy. When you have successfully raised your Boston Terrier around kids, it will be tolerant with other children, however, you need to have it supervised all the time.

- Can you handle the costs?

  Purchasing a purebred puppy is pricier than those who came from rescues or adult dogs. If price is an issue for you, you may consider adopting an adult dog.

- Would you like an old dog or rescued dog?

    If yes, you can open your heart and home to adopt an adult Boston Terrier. Many breeders will put their retired show dogs after the age of five years old.

These are the questions that you should ask you and yourself before you decide to get a puppy or an adult. Other than this, you may also need to consider your experience in raising a puppy, and also think of the future set-up or makeup of your family, activity level in your house.

Choosing a Puppy

If you plan to get a puppy, you need to ready yourself for some good fun! Having a puppy up to its adulthood will be one of the most rewarding experiences in your lifetime. You will watch your puppy grow up and then develop into a happy and healthy adult, aside from this, your dog will be easy to train and adaptable. You will have a lifetime of adoration and companionship from a Boston puppy.

You need to have very long hours of socializing and training for your puppy. You will have regular feeding hours for the dog within the day. Aside from this, you need to teach it to go to the bathroom and bond with it. You need to be aware of what you do in your house because it will affect your actions, such as its behavior and patterns throughout its life.

The Reputable Source

You can find purebred Boston Terrier puppies everywhere! It could be from online, breeders, or even your local pet stores. You may also find puppies listed in magazines and some are even listed in the newspaper. However, how would you know if the dealer or breeder is good? What is your assurance that the dog you will be getting is healthy, from great lineage, and knows how to socialize with other dogs? What is your assurance that your dog is of good temperament?

You may need to look for dealers and breeders who are expert in breeding, selecting, and preparing the puppies for happy homes. There are many breeders through different outlets, from individual breeders up to pet stores.

A good dog breeder will preserve and improve the breed that they love. A breeder would even stick to one breed to raise up. S/he is personally involve in dog shows and dog groups and even dog competitions. The goal of this breeder is to perfect the trait that will make the breed great.

What are the telltale signs of a reputable breeder?

- The breeder will choose the breeding dogs very carefully. S/he will have the goal to improve and preserve the breed of choice. S/he will also conform to the breed standard to produce the best puppies possible.

- S/he will test for defects and illnesses and will try its best to eliminate unhealthy signs of dog in the breeding program.

- S/he will provide you with proofs, such as health screening, plenty of references, and even a sales contract.

- The breeder won't commercialize the sale of the puppy. S/he will have a waiting list for the people who would want to purchase or get a puppy from him or her.

- The breeder will ask you about your personal details, such as its experience with dogs, home, lifestyle, and the goals with the puppy. The breeder might even ask you to complete an application form.

- The breeder will open up his/her home so you can inspect the breeding site. S/he will introduce you to the parents and litters and will also show you photos, health certificates, and pedigrees from both parents.

- The breeder would take the dog back if you can't provide a good home for the puppy anymore.

You can find breeders through local magazines or even a quick online search; however, you might even find a dog breeder through a kennel club or even a breed club. The Boston Terrier Club of America would list down members who follow a good conduct and code of ethics. Aside from this, you can even find dog breeders in dog shows. You may want to talk to the people during the show.

Here are some questions that you can ask your dog breeder:

- How long have you been breeding the Boston Terrier?
- Have you ever bred other dogs?

- Are you a member of any dog organizations?

- What is the history of the dog's parents? What are their strengths? Weaknesses?

- Can I visit your home and see the parents?

- Where do you raise the puppies?

- Have you socialized the puppies well?

- What health certificates do you have? Do you dogs have health problems?

- What kind of health guarantee do you have for your dogs?

- How many litters would you usually raise in a year?

- At what age can I take the puppy home?

BACKYARD BREEDERS AND PUPPY MILLS

These words have negative definitions. Some puppy mills and backyard breeders raise puppies as commodity and not as dog.

A backyard breeder breeds a dog to make some extra money. She may not have enough knowledge about selecting the best trait to prevent malformation.

A puppy mill is a facility to churn out puppies to make money. They could be farms or even in a residence.

Some may keep their animals in dirty, filthy, and inhumane conditions. The dogs from this place aren't really taken care of and not really happy.

PET STORES

Pet stores have a bad reputation when it comes to selling purebred dogs. They have smelly shops where puppies are kept in dirty, cramped kennels which is just inhumane for the dogs.

Some pet store owners may become excellent puppy breeders. S/he may scrutinize the puppy breeding and finding homes for the puppies. They keep their dogs in a sanitized happy area so it can socialize with other people and puppies. They would also question potential buyers, some may even require to fill out application form that will serve as a liaison between the buyer and the breeder.

Here are some questions that you can ask the shopkeeper:

- Who is the source of your Boston Terrier puppies?

- What is the background of these Boston Terrier puppies?

- Have you personally inspected the parents and the facilities of the puppies?

- Do you have an on-call veterinarian?

- How are you socializing the puppies?

- Can I thoroughly inspect the puppies?

- Can I inspect your facility?

- What is your guarantee policy?

- What information do you want from me?

Choosing an Adult

An adult Boston Terrier would make an excellent choice for you and your family if you do not want to endure the tiring puppy behaviors such as chewing, housetraining, and obedience training. There are a lot of healthy adult Boston Terriers in need of love and affection available around the country.

You can find adult Boston Terrier through breeders and kennel clubs. These dogs are past their reproductive stage and these dogs would spend their remaining number of years being spoiled by loving owners.

BREEDERS

You can also find excellent Boston Terriers through different breeders. There are many adult male or female terriers that have passed their reproductive era or some have flaws that would disqualify them from dog shows.

You can find these breeders on dog shows, from kennel clubs, searching through periodicals, or even asking your vet or friends for referral. Ask enough questions, visit their facility, and thoroughly inspect your do before leaving or buying your dog.

RESCUES

Rescued purebred dog are becoming more popular over the couple of years, because they dogs are being euthanized in shelters are also increasing. Several breed clubs and independent organization have formed rescue groups to save these animals and find new homes.

You can find Boston Terrier rescue groups in your area through contacting your regional humane society, animal control, vet, or even pet stores. Many of these places will provide you with rescue places.

These places will need you to complete an application and have an interview with a representative from the organization. When you are approved for the adoption, you will place into a waiting list or even told if there are dogs available. However, you will not get as much information about the dog as you would want from a breeder, but you will know if the dog is healthy and is already house trained.

When you have successfully adopted the dog, the group would conduct follow ups to make sure that the dog is settling okay with you. The rescue groups do not want to 'rescue' again the dog from you, so you need to take care of the dog throughout its life.

These are just some of the ways you can purchase or even adopt a puppy or an adult dog. Make sure you have enough information about the breeder so you will be assured of its quality

Chapter Four: Caring for Your Boston Terriers

You have now decided to welcome a Boston Terrier in your life, what now? Do you think your home is ready for your dog's arrival? What supplies would I need for the first few days? How could we schedule and delegate the chores for your new pet?

Your Boston Terrier is coming home to you and would want to explore new surroundings. The arrival of this dog would require some serious planning that would ensure the health, safety, and happiness. You need to put away all the puppy temptation in exchange for yummy dog food for your dog to survive and be well.

In this section, we will provide you with essential information for puppy-proofing and dog-proofing your yard and how. We would also give you the shopping list of the needed equipment during the homecoming. Aside from this, we will help you delegate tasks to family members in assigning dog chores.

Puppy Proofing 101

Preparing your yard and your house to a new puppy or dog is just similar for a curious toddler. Imagine you are a Boston Terrier – about 2 feet!

Your puppy or dog would want to investigate everything! Just like closet, electrical cord, and every rut your can find inside the house. It will not really distinguish between a chew toy and your most expensive pair of shoes.

In the following section, we will give you some puppy temptations that you will find both outside and inside of your house. When you remove the temptation when your dog comes home, you will surely know that your dog will succeed in life.

These things are just some of the things that your dog might come across in your new home. You need to inspect your home and yard thoroughly before your dog comes home, and you need to do this daily.

If you see that your dog has ingested something harmful or injures himself, you need to contact your vet immediately.

Keeping Things inside Your Home

There are a lot of things that become temptation to your puppy or dog when it reaches your home. There are many small puppies that would resemble playthings that would be a toy for your puppy. View the world from your dog's point of view and see look at the following areas:

KITCHEN

Your kitchen will contain a lot of interesting drawers, cords, and cabinets, as well as many tastes and smells. If you believe that your dog could go inside a drawer or a cabinet, you would be sure that your Boston Terrier would explore inside those places. Make sure you childproof your latches to prevent your dog from investigating off-limit areas and keep harmful foods away and cleaning supplies out of reach.

Aside from this, make sure to keep the power cords away from the dogs, power cords can be chew toys for teething Boston Terrier. You can enclose these power cords in a chew proof PVC tube.

Smells can be also a big temptation for the Boston Terrier. You need to be diligent in putting left-overs away in your fridge rather than just leaving it on the table. Make sure you also put a lock lid or store behind a latched cabinet your garbage can to keep your trash inside the can.

BATHROOM

Your bathroom, too, can be a dangerous place for your Boston Terrier. There are a lot of pills, soap, razors, and cotton swabs that could be left at your dog's reach which your dog could easily ingest and chew.

You also need to tell your family members to keep the bathroom clean after using it. You need to place your soaps, accessories, shampoos, and tissues away inside your drawer or cabinet.

When your Boston Terrier is still young, make it a habit to keep the toilet lid down at all times and make sure that the bathroom door is closed. Your pup could go in the bowl and drown. Same as the kitchen make sure that the trash can has a lock or stash it under a sink. Also, install childproof latches on the cabinets and drawers, and keep the dangling cords away.

BEDROOM

Dogs prioritize their sense of smell; they will go towards to anything that smells like you. Clothes, shoes, and slippers will easily become toys if you do not keep these items behind closed closet door. Make sure you keep your clothes off of the floor, shoes out of reach, and laundry in a closed hamper.

Aside from this, make sure you keep jewelries, coins, hair ties and other small items in containers or drawers. Make sure you also block the den under your bed as your dog might get stuck under it.

Outdoor Hazards

You also need to look at your yard and garage and see that there are many dangers for your Boston Terrier. Make sure you inspect and puppy - proof your home from your dog's perspective.

CHEMICALS AND POISONS

Cleaners, fertilizer, gasoline, painting, insecticides, and antifreeze are just some of the chemical and poisons that you have in your outside shed or even your garage.

Antifreeze has a sweet taste that could attract your animal, but it would be very deadly if your dog will ingest it

- even at small amounts. Make sure to secure boxes, bottles, and containers are secured and tucked away on locked cabinets doors or high places where your Boston Terrier can't reach.

Snail bait, rat poisons, and ant traps can be a tasty treat to your pup, but they really, they are not. So, you should put these away.

PLANTS

Any dog is a curious dog, and they would like to investigate anything that is new around it. They would want to dig up plants in the yard, especially if the dog is left unattended.

Daffodils, Birds of Paradise, foxglove, and lupine are just some plants that are poisonous to your dog and may cause varied reactions that vary from rash, diarrhea, and a rash. Place a fence around your plants and tell your dog where it can't be to protect both the plant and your dog.

GARDENING EQUIPMENT AND TOOLS

Your dog could cause accidents around your dogs. If your dog sniff sharp blade, it could cut its delicate nose, or may tug a cord that would cause a heavy saw that could fall from a high place and injure your dog.

Let's Shop!

You need to shop for the needs of your furry friend, but could be intimidating! Walking through aisles after aisles in a big-box retailer, pet boutique, or any local department store that would contain food, treats, beds, toys, and some doggy couture could surely shock you!

You may want to splurge your money for your dog. But do not worry; you will have a lot of time to do that. You need to pick up a few items first before your dog comes home.

Collars, Leashes – What shall I get?!

You need to provide your Boston Terrier a harness, collar, and leash especially when your dog comes home. In this section, you will learn all about these things.

COLLARS

A collar has both the stylish function and fashion statement. It contains a lot of information about your dog, such as its licensing tag, and it's ID, which contains your information when your dog gets lost. The collar, is then, attached to the leash, which you can use to walk your Boston.

For its initial collar, you may want to pick up an adjustable nylon type with a buckle that comes with a lot colors and styles that would fit your Boston Terrier's personality.

You need to measure your dog's neck and add two inches to add some room to grow, to find the right size; or, you may bring your dog to the pet store and try the collar to your dog. You will buy several collars when your dog grows up.

When your dog has fully become an adult, there are a lot of decorative collar choices! You can buy diamond leather collar, studded collar, or even colorful vinyl collar! You may even buy several collars to celebrate season.

Whatever style and kind you choose, make sure you choose the correct weight and size for your Boston Terrier. Big heavy collars are pretty harmful to your dogs, and may even choke your dog.

Some other collars are designed for training purposes, such as choke collars or slip chains. But make sure you buy it when your dog is already grown up, especially with the help of your vet or a professional trainer.

LEASHES

The leash is attached to the collar, which you can use to control the Boston Terrier during obedience training or walks. You can choose coordinating colors and designs for your leashes and collars. When you buy your leash, make sure the leash that you buy won't unhook or break from the collar. Aside from this, choose one that is comfortable and strong for your hand. There are a lot of styles, lengths, and materials for your leash collars. Find one that best suits your purpose.

HARNESSES

If you are not fan of collars, you may opt to buy harnesses. A harness will be looped around his torso and shoulder. You can use both the collar and harness interchangeably, but a harness will be suitable for your Boston especially when walking. A harness will give you less control of your dog, but will prevent your dog from choking or gasping.

BOWLS!

Your Boston Terrier needs food and water for its daily need. A way for you to suffice your dog's need is through the food and water bowl. There are many designs and material for your doggy water and food dishes. Some might be ceramic, pottery, stainless steel, plastic, and others. In this portion, we will be discussing the benefits of drawback of your food bowl and water bowl:

PLASTIC BOWLS

- Lightweight

- Inexpensive

- Retain residue and harbor bacteria

- Your dog might chew and swallow the little plastic pieces

CERAMIC PIECES

- weigh more, so it won't be tipped over or turned like a toy.

- More expensive

- breakable

- If they are made overseas, it may contain lead which is harmful to any animal.

STAINLESS STEEL

- most expensive

- easy to clean and sanitize

- virtually indestructible

Your dog will need two sets of bowls, so you need to clean and rotate the usage of the bowls of regularly.

How Do I Keep Your Boston Terrier contained?

It is a must for you as an owner is having containment devices to keep your Boston Terrier in a confined area where you can house train and monitor it.

There are three categories for the dog's carrier:

- Travel carrier or crate

  It can be used as a den which can be used in the car, home, or airplane.

- Around-town tote

  It can transport your dog into different establishments.

- Pet purse

  It looks like a handbag which you can use to take your pet in different places such as theaters and restaurants.

You can also provide playpens, X-pens, and baby gates for curious, growing puppies. These are also short term solution if you are unable to keep your eyes to your Boston Terrier.

Chapter Five: Welcoming Your New Dog Home

Today is the day that your Boston Terrier goes home! You have already a lot of supplies and puppy-proofed the house, you have provided every need, starting from buying the perfect crate up to the newest collar-leash combo! But now, the real battle and fun activity begin!

When you welcome an adult dog or puppy into your home, the new activities will never stop! Your loving and intelligent Boston Terrier will entertain you all day long! It will also challenge you and push you to your limits as soon as the dog walks through your home. In order to keep your relationship alive, you need to impose house rules to know where the dog is allowed, what she is allowed to do, and how she is expected to act.

Aside from this, you also need to set up rules for the humans in the household. Using regular routines and consistent house technique, you and your family could teach your Boston Terrier how to be a great and important part of your family.

Your home is a new environment for your dog. This will be an intimidating scene for your Boston Terrier, which would make the strongest dog quiver. In this portion, we will be discovering ways on how to make a welcoming environment for your dog, as well as introducing to new surroundings, and establishing house rules for the Boston Terrier and your family members.

If you have a work schedule from Monday through Friday, it is best to bring home your pup on a Friday afternoon or even Saturday morning. You need to spend several days together with your new Boston Terrier. You need, first, to establish routine for going to the bathroom, feeding, and playing.

TAKING THE HOME TOUR

When your dog first arrives home, you need to show your Boston Terrier around your house. You need to focus on places where it is important for your dog, especially her drinking and eating places, play area, sleeping space, and bathroom spot.

When your Boston Terrier is still a puppy, you need to limit the number of rooms your dog has access to, if you do this, it will make your Boston Terrier secure and safe, and it will teach your pup about boundaries. When the dog matures, you need to expand the universe to include other areas of the house and let the dog roam around the house, but you need to supervise the dog from room to room.

Before you let the dog enter the house, you need to give chance to your dog to relieve herself in the yard. In this way, you will have peace of mind so your do won't have an accident when she explores and sniff new areas in your house.

YOUR DOG'S DRINKING AND EATING AREA

In this area, your Boston Terrier eats and fills her belly with delicious food. This will be one of her favorite spots in her life.

You need to find a logical space to put your dog's food and water bowls, either in the kitchen, laundry room, garage, or even in an out-of-the-way spot, especially if you have small space.

When you have decided where you serve your dog's meals, you need to let your family know where the designated area for your dog's dining area is.

You need to introduce the area immediately when your dog comes home, you need to use a lot of enthusiasm and praise. If your dog loves to eat, let her. If she is not eating yet, let her too. It might be because your dog is too excited and nervous at the same time.

SLEEPING AND DEN AREA

Your dog's crate will act as your Boston Terrier's sleeping area and den. It can be made out of hard plastic or even a powder-coated metal. This place will be your dog's cave, make sure to make it as safe place where your dog could enjoy some "me" time.

During mornings, you need to place our Boston Terrier inside the crate with the door closed to train your dog to hold the bladder. Your dog will not pee where they sleep, this will teach your dog to wait until you take your dog outside.

With the door open, this crate will serve as your dog's personal space. Your dog will use it as a hiding place when she feels like she is taking a nap and a safe space when there are strangers coming over. During nights, you need put the dog inside the crate until you dog is old enough.

If you are using a different crate from the one you used to bring the dog home, introduce the dog where you kept it. If you are using the same create, you need to set it up on a particular spot in the house. Put it on a specific space and make sure you introduce your dog where it is placed.

When considering the where you keep the crate, ask the questions:

- Where do you, as the owner, spend a lot of time?

- Will you provide another crate in another place?

- Are there many draft inside the area?

- Is the area easy to clean?

PLAY AREAS

Boston Terriers really love to play; you should allot an area for safe and fun play activity. When your Boston Terrier is still young, it does not really need so much space, having a playpen is enough. However, when your dog is growing up, it may need more room to play, you need to have more area to play in, such as in the living room and bedroom.

You need to keep the toys there, identify the play area to the pup especially when it is young. You need to let her play with some toys in the space.

You need to decide where is the most suitable area for your dog to freely play in. Make sure that the area is easy to clean, does not contain expensive furniture or have harmful and dangerous plants. The place should also be a place where the family gather, and the crate should be around the area.

Meeting the Members of the Family

You need to welcome the pup to the family through introducing to the other members of the pack; this includes other pets and other children. You need to have discipline and training so that integrating the Boston Terrier in the household.

KID MEETING 101

If you have children, nephew, nieces, or any kid that comes to your home frequently, it probably is very excited to meet the Boston Terrier!

Most kids love to cuddle and play with puppies, but this behaviour could be too much for your dog to handle. Children who do not know how to handle pets may hurt the puppy instead of giving it love. In this portion, we will help you prevent accidental injury or overstimulation of the kids and the puppy. We will divide the section into two, one for the kids, another one for the puppy.

Children who have not yet seen or played with other dogs need more care during the first few months. You need to tell them never go near a strange dog, especially if there is no adult present in the place.

If they already know the dog, tell the children not to put the face too near to their face or tease the animal. Do not, ever, frighten a child, but let them know that some dogs may behave unexpectedly.

TINY CHILDREN

Toddlers and preschool-aged kids will believe that your dog is just another fuzzy stuffed animal! It may think that the dog is an interactive play thing that would give them too much entertainment. However, Boston Terriers are not toys. If you handled them improperly, your dog could be seriously injured.

Here are some steps into introducing your tiny tots to your Boston Terrier:

- Ask the child to slowly approach the Boston when you are sitting on the floor and hold the puppy in your arms.

- Show the child to how to properly handle, model the behaviour to the child to allow the child to mimic the movement. Slowly ask the child to pet the puppy.

- If the child wants to hold the puppy, make sure you sit on the floor and gently place the dog on his or her lap. Make sure to tell the child to just touch the puppy gently.

- Watch both the child's and dog's body language. If anyone cries or squirms, make sure that the playtime is over.

- After the playtime is over, make sure you go over the rules again.

GRADE SCHOOL KIDS

Kids this age would want to run, cuddle, and play with the puppy. When your Boston Terrier is older, these games are okay. But if they are meeting for the first time, the dog might be shocked to these antics. Follow these rules for the first interactions:

- Ask the child to sit and wait for further instructions. Make sure that you tell him not to run or hug the dog immediately.

- Let the child approach the dog slowly. The pup will sniff the dog.

- When the dog is done sniffing, ask the child to extend one hand for the dog to smell. Tell the child that this is the appropriate way to introduce himself or herself to the dog.

- Make sure that every play time is supervised, so you can know that their play is not too rough or exuberantly.

- Tell the child that the dog's nose, eyes, and mouths are off-limits and are prone to injure. Teach the child how to handle the dog properly and with extreme care.

These are just some things that you need to know especially during the first few days when you welcome the dog at your home

Chapter Six: Eating Tips for Your Boston Terrier

Your Boston Terrier's diet will give it the necessary energy to make it through a busy and fun-filled day. These dogs have a hearty appetite that requires a healthy diet with the correct amount of fats, minerals, carbohydrates, protein, and vitamins per serving.

There are many kinds of food available at many different choices, but what shall you choose? In this chapter, we will explore different brands that vary in sizes and prices, as well as both dry and wet food covered with gravy.

We will also help you out in creating your Boston Terrier's diet from scratch. You need to figure out what suits your Boston Terrier the best. Aside from this, figure out the correct diet and eating schedule that suitable for the age. The proper nutrition will help your Boston Terrier be the very best pup it can be.

Cost vs. Quality

Before dogs became domesticated animals, they scavenged and preyed on small animals. They searched for food, eating berries, grains, and other plants wherever they can.

This diet gives them the necessary minerals, carbohydrate, protein, vitamins, and fats for a complete and healthy diet. For Boston Terriers, they require these basic nutrients. However, the dogs have different requirements based on the age. Young and growing puppies need a diet that is suitable for growth, while adults need a formulation suited for maintenance.

The price of the food depends well on the brand of the dog food. Even though most dog manufacturers follow basic guidelines, the 'premium' products are more expensive and may exceed specifications for your dog. The higher the food grate, the fewer the fillers, the better the taste.

Premium brands contain added nutrients such as vitamin supplements and antioxidants that would benefit several kinds of dogs such as overweight dogs, senior dogs, or even for specific breeds.

In short, you truly get what you pay for. However, do not presume the most expensive is the better. Make sure you also ask your vet to choose the best diet for your dog.

Knowing the Ingredients

Dog require specific amounts of carbohydrates, vitamins, protein, fat, and minerals to have normal body function. In this part, we will closely look at the required nutrients to make sure your Boston Terrier will become happy and healthy.

GIVE ME SOME PROTEIN

Your Boston Terrier needs protein for developing and growing skin and hair, producing hormones, having muscle mass, healing damaged tissues, and regulating metabolism.

Protein is the first ingredient for many premium dog food brands. Chicken, lamb, beef, turkey, or duck are the proteins mostly used by the dog food companies. However, some might even use fish meal, eggs, milk products, fish, liver, and milk.

Some companies might even use grain and beans, such as wheat, barley, soy, rice, and corn. However, these are not complete protein sources unlike animal protein. But, if they are combined with other types of food, this could provide a lot of amino acids that your dog requires.

Boston Terrier pups need about 28% protein, while Boston Terrier adults need around 22% protein. Do not pick one based alone on the formula's protein percentage. Remember, the protein source matters. In lower priced food, lesser grade protein is more difficult for the dog to digest.

BUILD ENERGY WITH CARBS

Carbohydrates are the sugar and starches found in plant foods. This provides quick boosts of energy for Boston Terrier needed for their play and exercise. About 50% if your dog's diet is carbohydrates, which also provide fiber which is needed for correct bowel function. Some other sources of fibers are grains, pasta, potatoes, rice, and even peas.

Unfortunately, carbohydrates are also fillers. Why? Because these things are cheaper than protein, so the manufacturers tend to use rice and corn to bulk up the food at a cheaper and lower price.

Premium foods, however, contain high-quality yet complex carbohydrates to give your dog sustained energy and dog fiber.

If there are many cereal grains in the food, this would hype up your Boston Terrier. Your dog would be bouncing off the walls and play without ceasing. If you do not want this to happen, make sure you get the correct type of carbohydrate for the diet, but still limit it. Make sure there are little to no fillers for your dog food.

WANT SHINY COAT AND ENERGY? GET FATS!

Oils and fats do more than make your food taste better. Both oils and fats provide energy that would help your Boston Terrier feel very satisfied.

Fats are also used to break down vitamins such as vitamin A, K, E, and D. Some forms of fat also support and give skin and coat health. This will make your Boston Terrier's short coat shiny and attain more shimmer.

If you see that your Boston Terrier's coat is looking dull, give food that has a high percentage of unsaturated fat.

If the dog is a little bit overweight, talk to your vet to switch to a low-fat diet.

VITAMINS AND MINERALS, PLEASE!

Your Boston Terrie would also require vitamins which will help the dog fight diseases, regulate metabolism, absorb minerals, and grow and function normally.

Animal and plant food contain vitamins. Your dog's body will maintain and store fat-soluble vitamin in the body's fatty and liver tissues, water-soluble vitamins, such as vitamins B and C. These things are flushed out daily, which must be replaced.

Reading Pet Food Labels

As a human, we tend to look at the food labels for the food that we eat. The labels contain basic information about the item, such as the calories, ingredients, and nutrient content. Every dog label is different.

Pet foods are also regulated by the Food and Drug Administration Center. Here are the breakdowns of the info in the food label:

- **Feeding Instruction**

  These are the guidelines for you to know how much you need to feed your Boston Terrier, depending on his weight.

  If the food is formulated for puppies, it will give information based on its age. Sometimes, so companies may even give information on how often you need to feed your dog.

- **Ingredients**

  The ingredients in the pet food are listed in descending order by amount. Often, the protein appears first, followed by grains, fats, additives, and preservatives.

- **Manufacturer's Contact Information**

  The name and contact information of the packer, manufacturer or distributor are required. Sometimes, the manufacturers include a toll-free number, site address, but are not really mandatory.

- **Statement of Nutritional Adequacy**

  The nutritional adequacy statement will tell us whether the food will provide complete and balanced nutrition for a dog based on nutritional level based on the AAFCO.

  The statement written on the label will provide a life stage claim for which the food is intended.

- **Guaranteed Analysis**

  This analysis will break down by percentage especially what nutrients are in the food. It lists down minimum level of crude fat and crude protein. It also gives measurement or percentage of vitamins, additives, and minerals.

Armed with this great knowledge and the nutritional guideline we have previously given, you now know how to read the food label confidently.

Feed Me!

Boston Terrier are considered as small dog, so they do not require big amount of food. Boston Terrier only eat a small or lesser amount of food, in this light, the quality matters when you are feeding your baby dog. You need to give a delicious diet that will meet the dog's nutritional needs, such as carbs, vitamins, minerals, protein, and fats.

Luckily, there are a lot of places to offer a variety of dog food, such as pet stores and vet office. Soon, you will find a formula suited for your puppy that will make it healthy. Here is the overview of the different diet you can give to your pet:

DRIED KIBBLE

These crunchy little dog food are formulated that contains all the nutrition your Boston Terrier needs. It comes in a wide variety of formula and flavors with a lot of nutritional sources.

Whatever food you choose, make sure you give quality recipe that has carbohydrates, protein, and fats that came from easily digestible sources.

The food's shape, texture, taste, size, and smell are well researched and tested by vet nutritionist and even scientist. These people have devoted their time and energy to produce recipes, conduct feeding trials, and balance the nutritional values to ensure that the food will agree to the FDA standard. Luckily, your Boston Terrier digest these food easily.

SEMI-MOIST

This kind of food resembles a moist clay texture. This food contains balanced nutrition. This food contains higher water content that the dried kibble variant. These semi-moist food has higher sugar content which could cause tartar and plaque buildup on a dog's teeth, which would lead to tooth decay. This food is best served as a treat rather than daily food intake.

Like the kibbles, these foods are formulated to meet the nutritional needs of the dog. Semi-moist food is somehow better for kibbles due to its water content. Your senior dog or those with dental problem would surely love to chew these foods. This variant is also more appealing to your picky eater.

CANNED FOOD

Dogs love meaty stew! Canned diets are a close relative of "real" food. This food is often packed with potatoes, lots of gravy, carrots, and chunks of meat! This diet will provide a complete nutrition, tempting meal for picky eaters, and a great amount of water.

ORGANIC OR NATURAL

This is a popular diet for your dog, many formula need ingredients from organic farms that claim to have "human-quality" ingredient.

This is actually a great food diet of Boston Terrier, however, you need to get them from reputable source.

RAW FOOD

Raw diet is just that. It means that you will feed your pet raw meat. These meals are found in the pet store's freezer case. If you will have this kind of diet, you need to consult your vet first.

This kind of diet lack necessary nutrients such as minerals and vitamins that are found in plant-based foods, so you need to add more to your dog's meal to have enough nutrition for better health.

HOME MADE DELICACIES

Some people actually prefer to prepare their dog's food from scratch. There are a few dog food cookbooks on the market that contains mouthwatering recipes for your dog.

You need to consult first your vet before offering this type of diet to your dog, especially to know how to attain enough nutritional requirements for your dog.

Before you feed your Boston Terrier a homemade diet, answer these following questions:

- Do you have enough time to prepare food for your dog?

  Preparing for homemade dog food is just like cooing another member of the family.

- Does your fridge have space to store raw meat or meals?

    Because these foods are fresh, you need to store these to the freezer or refrigerator.

- Do you travel a lot? Or do a lot of work?

    If you travel a lot, this might not be the option for you. Dog sitters or boarding center won't make your dog dinner every night.

- Is there a reliable butcher near you? Can you get fresh, organic meat?

    If you know someone that can provide you with fresh meat, this is a go. Make sure that you know this person to know if this is organic or not.

- Have you researched thoroughly about the dog's nutritional need?

    You need to research and learn all about dog nutrition. Ask help from your vet to outline meals and supplements to be added to the meal.

PRESCRIPTION

This type of diet is purchased through vet office, this option is suitable for dogs that may have allergies or need special nutritional requirements. Visit your vet immediately to prescribe the best food for your pup.

Yummy Cuisines for Your Boston Terriers

When it comes to treats and food for your Boston, you can choose from a lot of things! From crunchy dog food and canned stews, organic blends from human food, and other.

DIET

When your Boston Terrier is still young, it requires food formulated specifically for development and growth. It needs to have essential nutrients such as carbohydrates and proteins that will encourage the growth of health muscles and bones.

When it reaches adulthood, the dog will need food that is specifically designed for maintenance. Selecting the right food and right diet is difficult. You can feed the same diet that your breeder fed your Boston to prevent the change of stomach. However, your Boston Terrier will be the one to choose its diet. If it does not like the food, it will not eat it!

TREATS

You can feed your dog with the traditional biscuit; you can also give freeze-dried meat! You need to visit downtown doggy bakery to order some freshly baked and yummy cookies. You can even bake your own treats!

When choosing the teats, make sure to note the ingredients and nutritional information so you know what food is your pup is ingesting. It might be tempting to give treats to your dog often but remember that these things are treats and not meals. Too much treats would lead to a weight issue.

These are just some of the things that you need to know about feeding your pet. Make sure you know these things before you run off to the pet store or supermarket. Know your pet before giving any food.

Chapter Seven: Grooming Your Pet

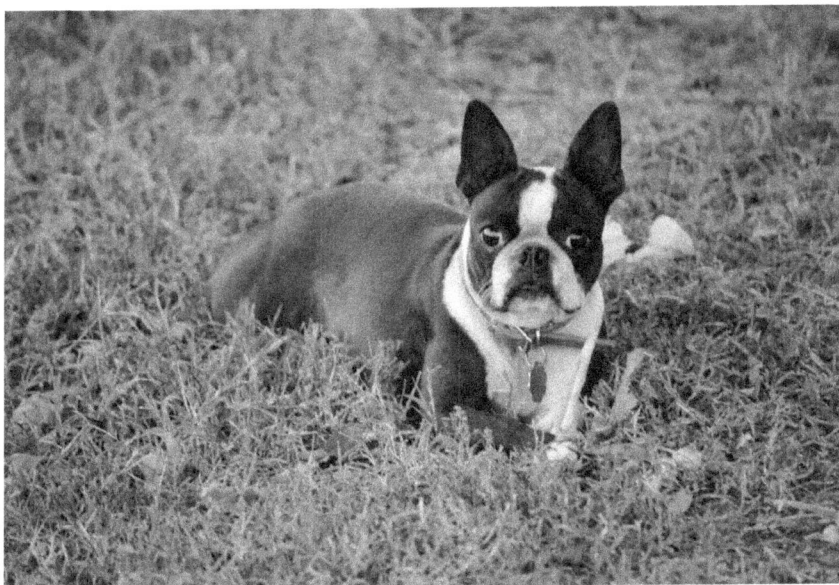

Because your dog is single-coated and short haired, Boston Terriers doesn't really need labor - intensive grooming process unlike some breeds. But, the dog still need regular brushing, washing, and nail trimming. Aside from this, your dog will need tooth brushing, ear cleaning in order your dog to be healthy and smelling really fresh.

Aside from the nails, ears, eyes, and teeth, keeping the coat will require great maintenance work. There are daily, weekly, semi-monthly grooming procedures that you need to do to minimize shedding and to keep the coat clean and glossy.

You need to figure out the tools and how to use them, grooming time may be difficult at first, but it will be a pleasurable experience for both you and your Boston Terrier. It will result a strong bond that would last forever.

Some skills might require a professional groomer. You need to choose one that makes you the most comfortable, this will require you to visit, research, and recommend from reliable sources. In this section, we will elp you select the best groomer possible.

Looking Good at Home

Just like humans, dog needs to bathe, comb hair, brush teeth daily. This will require routine maintenance to keep the coat lustrous and clean.

Your Boston Terrier also needs a visit to the groomer, and this will pamper the dog well, too! For daily upkeep, you can groom the dog yourself with just a few tools, with little instructions, and using only a couple of minutes throughout the day.

These small grooming rituals will also give you the opportunity to inspect and handle your beloved Boston Terrier. You can also check for abnormalities such as cuts and bumps. Other than this, you can also check the condition of your dog's eyes, mouth, paws, ears, and nose.

In this part, we will give you all the information you need in order to groom your Boston Terrier at the comfort of your own home. You will also discover a great set-up for the grooming area. Other than that, we will also give you the tools that you need and find out how to clean the pup's eyes, teeth, ears, and nose. We will help you develop a routine for the whole process such as scheduling the grooming process through the day, week, and pup that will make your pup cuddly and squeaky clean.

Ready, set, go!

Many breeders start grooming their pets when they are still young. What they do is hold and coddle them, look at their mouths, paws, eyes, and ears.

Probably, when you met your Boston Terrier, it is used to being handled and cuddled by humans. You need to continue the breeder's work by handling your Boston Terrier daily. Your dog needs to feel comfort when someone touches its body, inspecting its eyes, tickling its toes, and even rubbing the gums.

Before you begin the grooming process, you need to set-up a regular space, gather all the needed tools, and slowly introduce the dog into the grooming tradition.

THE RIGHT LOCATION

To begin the home beauty routine a.k.a doggy grooming 101, you need to find a specific location. Dogs like regular things; you need to choose one place wherein the dog will know what will happen and how to behave while you are grooming the dog.

Some people use their counter top whenever they clean and brush their Boston Terrier. Other owners use a grooming table which will let them have flexibility while they leave their dog to get the other tools. In whatever place you may choose, make sure you put a nonslip pad on the surface, and never, ever, leave your dog for a long time.

When choosing the correct place for your grooming station, make sure the area is near a tub or sink, where you can use a hand-held sprayer. You may also want a space with electrical outlet.

GATHER UP!

Here are the tools that you need:

- Shampoo and Conditioner

- Slicker Brush

- Bristle Brush

- Shedding Blade

- Soft Towel

- Scissors

- Nail Clippers

- Styptic Powder

- Cotton Balls

- Ear-cleaning solution

- Toothbrush and dog toothpaste

You can find all these things at shops near you such as local pet store supply, even online, or through a trusty groomer.

Healthy Skin and Coat

The tight and short Boston Terrier coat is really beautiful, and you need to keep it to look its best, you need to do some daily brushing and even monthly washing.

Your Boston Terrier only has a single-coat, which means it has no undercoat to keep the dog warm. It might get too chilly during cold months, however, this single coat means less grooming process for you. You do not need de-matting tool, undercoat rake, or even a de - shedding comb. You do not need to tease out knots or mats.

DAILY BRUSHING

When you start brushing your dog, you need to stick to the same routine every time you brush your dog.

You can follow these steps:

1. Put your Boston Terrier on its designated grooming place. Begin the brushing by using the bristle brush to smooth the coat down and remove any debris or dirt.

2. Feel any cuts, bumps, scrapes, or irregularities when you are brushing the dog.

3. Use the shedding blade to remove any dead hair.

4. When you have removed almost all the dead hair, use a slicker brush to remove any more excess.

MONTHLY BATH TIME

Your Boston Terrier will require semi-monthly or even monthly baths depending on your dog's level of activity and energy. If you exceed more than a month, it will dry out the skin and may cause brittle hair and even dandruff. Shampooing your dog's hair will not only remove dirt, but also, it washes away the natural oils in order to keep the coat shiny and clean.

Only use a shampoo and conditioner formulated for dogs when you are bathing your Boston Terrier. The conditioner is actually an optional step, it softens the coat, this is not really necessary but it will make your Boston Terrier more huggable and lovable.

Before beginning bath time, prepare all the things to wash, dry and brush your dog. You need to prepare conditioner, bristle brush, fluffy towels, shampoo, cotton balls, and the blow-drying.

Here are the steps that you can follow:

1. Brush your Boston Terrier's coat thoroughly before bath time.

2. Prepare all the things and the bathing area. Put the nonslip mat on the sink and place the conditioner, shampoo, and towels on an accessible place.

3. Plug the Boston Terrier's ears with cotton balls and put it near the sink.

4. Using lukewarm water, you rinse your dog's body and head; do not put any water into the ear. When your dog is thoroughly wet, turn off the water immediately.

5. Using a generous amount of shampoo, wash and massage the dog's hair and skin, you need to include the belly, ears, and rear.

6. Rinse thoroughly and completely the soap, work start from the head, down the back, and underneath the body.

7. Put conditioner as per manufacturer's instruction. Let it soak and rinse thoroughly.

8. Let the dog shake off the excess water then wrap your clean pup with a big fluffy towel to soak up the rest.

9. Use a blow-dryer in the low or no-heat setting. Be careful around the face, neck, and even the tails.

Paw - Dicure 101

Nail trimming is a grooming procedure that you should do monthly. You will know when your Boston Terrier's nails too long if you hear clicking sounds whenever it walks on the floor!

The ideal time for nail trimming is when it is softened by warm water. Just like any living being, the dog's toenails will continue to grow so it needs to be trimmed to keep them at a healthy length. To cut the Boston Terrier's nail, you need to:

1. Put the dog in a position that is both comfortable for the two of you.

2. Get help to securely place your dog, hold the trimmers with your dominant hand the dog's paw using the other hand.

3. Press your index finger and thumb on a toe, which would extend the nail and prevent it from retracting.

4. Clip off the portion of the nail that you see is curving downward.

5. Repeat with the other toes.

Ear Cleaning 101

Follow these steps to clean your Boston Terrier's ears:

- Inspect the outer portion of your Boston Terrier's ear. Hold the edge of the ear and check for discharge, signs of ear mites, wax, and even odor.
- Use a cotton ball that is already moistened with ear cleaning solution; wipe the inside of the ear, making sure that you get all the part of it.
- Use a new, fresh cotton ball for the other ear.
- Make sure you thoroughly dry the ears using a new, clean, and dry cotton ball.

These are things that you need to consider whenever you are grooming your Boston Terrier. It may be difficult at first, but you will get a hang of it as time goes by.

Chapter Eight: Visiting Your Veterinarian

Your Boston Terrier could not really take care of itself, particularly on the health aspect. One of the things that you need to do is have a good relationship with a vet that you will trust, someone you can ask questions, share concerns, and call at odds times when the unthinkable happens. You and your vet need to work together to have a long and healthy life for your loving dog.

In this portion, we will give you a run down on how find a qualified vet. We will also give you an insight on what will happen during your very first vet visit, including the vaccinations that your puppy might need.

Finding the Best Vet for Your Pet

The vet will be the one who will keep your Boston Terrier protected against diseases and still be healthy. She or she will conduct annual screening and will suggest preventive care that will ensure that your Boston Terrier a healthy and long life.

The vet will also vaccinate your dog against common diseases, perform necessary treatments, prescribe remedies, and may address your concerns or questions you may have. In total, the vet will become your dog's best friend.

Look for a vet before you welcome your Boston Terrier enters your family. You need to have a doctor-patient-pet owner relationship immediately, and it will start with knowing who the best vet for you is.

Refer the Best Vet, Please?

You can find the best vet in the area through local Boston Terrier club, and may seek recommendation to several people. Good vets are suggested by club members because they rely to these people to take care of their pets. The vet needs to understand the breed and recommend treatments for your dog.

Here are the other sources for your vet:

- breeder
  - If your chosen breeder lives near you, he or she might be able to recommend a vet for you.
  - If the chosen breeder lives far, he or she might know someone who lives near you.

- family, friends, and other dog owners
  - First - hand accounts will help you on the vet's expertise and bedside manner! You can also see if their pets approved of the vet.

- vet associations
  - There are a lot of vet associations who will give you lists of vets around your area.
  - Some groups might even give you appointments to personally meet the vet.

- advertisement
  - Some vets like to advertise their clinic; this option would be for those who are not familiar with their area.
  - Focus only on the people near you

Who's who in the Vet World

Just like any other doctors, vets worked hard to earn their doctorate degrees and will go on practice as a general practitioner. The general practitioner will maintain your Boston Terrier's medical history, it will also perform routine exams such as minor surgeries, and can handle emergencies. In short, the GP is your Boston Terrier's primary doctor.

Here is the difference between the general practitioner and vet specialists:

GENERAL PRACTITIONER

Vets are generally licensed through the American Veterinary Medical Association (AVMA). They need to complete four years in AVMA-accredited vet school with a year dedicated to vet rotations. After this, they need to pass several exams on the federal and state levels to earn their licenses, then the, Doctor of Veterinary Medicine (DVM) or a Veterinary Medical Doctor (VMD). This well depends on the vet school that they have attended.

This kind of doctor is able to perform several services for your Boston Terrier. This will include vaccinations, diagnostics, annual check - ups, minor surgeries, and even prevention. If you think the Boston Terrier is sick, you first need to go through a general practitioner. But if your general practitioner decides that your Boston Terrier needs specialized care, you need to refer the dog to a specialists.

Vets practice their work in different settings, from big vet hospitals where there a lot of privately owned clinics wherein there are a lot doctors available. However, some doctors only work in franchise-like settings, and other are in teaching hospitals at vet schools.

SPECIALISTS

Vet specialists, such as vet behaviorists, dentists, surgeons, undergo another set of training after being a general practitioner. They chose to focus on a particular area of expertise.

In order for a person to be a vet specialist, the person must complete the first vet school program and earn the DVM. Then, that person should continue education through completing another year of internship and a two to five year residency program in the chosen field. After finishing the educational requirements, he or she must pass additional exams to be certified by specialty board.

What Do I Really Need?

In choosing the right vet and clinic where you bring your Boston Terrier, this actually depends on may criteria. If you research your own physician, you, too, should also research about your dog's vet and animal hospital.

Ask yourself the following questions:

- Do I need to find the vet near my home?
- What services would I need from the clinic or hospital?
- What doctor-patient-pet owner relationship do I want?
- Is good hospital or clinic staff important to me?

In the upcoming sections we will help you come up with the answers to these questions.

QUALITY OVER YOUR CONVENIENCE

Choosing the clinic or hospital near your home is surely convenient. You and your furry friend would easily show up to routine exam, groom visits, booster shots because your vet's office is just near your home.

The hours of the clinic or hospital should be compatible with your own schedule. Personally ask your doctor if they accommodate early or late appointment and if they area willing to see patients on the weekend.

However, do not only base your decision on your convenience because the nearest vet may not be a good fit for you. Both you and your dog should feel comfortable with the doctor and his or her skills, if you are hesitant, it is best to find someone else.

THE FULL PACKAGE

Vet clinics give wide range of services, starting from grooming up to boarding, ultrasound, and cancer treatment. Some vets even stock their shelves with products needed by your pets. Think of it as a department store, for your pet!

Before you select your clinic or hospital, note all the services which are needed by you and your pet. If you want to groom the pet by your own, grooming services might not be important. However, if you want to have a reliable dog sitter, you need to have boarding services.

You also need to know how the clinic or hospital handles the emergencies. Some places have staff such as vets and their nurses on call 24 hours a day, while some clinics do not have after hour's emergency.

You also need to ask if the clinic has a laboratory in the office or if they can send to the lab the needed materials. You need to talk to your vet or office manager about the length of time it will take to get lab results; you would not want to wait for days to figure out what is wrong with your loving Boston Terrier.

Also note if the clinic has specialty practitioner and services, such as oncologists (cancer doctors), behaviorists, or dentists. Some doctors can refer you to specialists, but you may need to have specialists near you.

ONE DOCTOR OVER A TEAM

In small clinics, there are only a handful of vets that you can see. In others, there is only one. This practice will maintain a great relationship between the doctor and pet. Your Boston Terrier will be happy and be comfortable in any treatment it will do.

HELPFUL OFFICE STAFF

The receptionist, nurses, and vet technicians are some other people that make up the vet's office. The quality and attentiveness of these people greatly affects the quality of your Boston Terrier's care.

The people in the front office should be both helpful and considerate. They need to greet you with a big smile when you arrive and readily schedule follow up appointments when needed.

Vet technicians or assistants should take your Boston Terrier's weight, vital signs, and temperature before the doctor arrives in the exam room. They might even be the one to explain the doctor's diagnosis in simpler terms.

Are We Ready for Alternatives?

Other than the traditional vet care, you can also complement alternative health care for your Boston Terrier. Some alternatives include acupressure, chiropractic, acupuncture, and massage care.

Both the acupuncture and acupressure are Eastern therapies consisting of stimulation of the precise points within your dog's body. This is done through the insertion of fine needles and/or applying pressure. Some vets are trained for doing this type of therapy.

Massaging and chiropractic therapy is done through working the animal's muscles and skeletal system to ease the pain and speed healing. If you prefer to do this task, you need to ask your vet first for his or her recommendation, and for more information.

These are just some important information when choosing your vet. It might be difficult to select the best vet at first; you may even go through a trial and error method. But you need to find the best that would treat your Boston Terrier with love and great understanding.

Chapter Nine: Boston Terrier as Show Dogs

Aside from being wonderful companion, Boston Terrier could be shown at different dog shows. They are very easy to train through hard work and perseverance, so you can train them for basic commands at first then moving on to complex ones. However, before you go off and research on different dog shows, make sure you read this chapter about the breed standards. Both the American Kennel Club and United Kingdom Kennel Club have set their guidelines into what kind of dog is acceptable in their shows. Skim through this chapter and compare your dog's characteristics – if it fit, go out and research about different Boston Terrier dog shows!

Showing Off Your Dogs

You could not really just barge in and enter your dog into a dog show. Being in a dog show is a painstaking process that will require you to devote your time, energy and patience into forming the best dog possible. Make sure your dog meet the breed standards set by the AKC.

BOSTON TERRIER BREED STANDARD

General Appearance:

- lively
- highly intelligent
- smooth coated
- short - headed
- compactly built
- short-tailed
- well balanced dog,
- Brindle, seal or black in color and evenly marked with white.
- The size of the head is in proportion with the size of the dog.
- The dog's expression shows a high degree on intelligence.
- The Boston Terrier's body is simply short and well knit.

- Its limbs are neatly turned and strong.
- The dog's tail is short
- No feature is very prominent that the dog may appear weirdly proportionate.
- The dog gives an impression of strength, determination, and activity.
- It displays an easy and graceful carriage and a high order of style
- There is a balance of expression and color of white markings.

Size, Proportion, Substance:

- There are different divisions that are divided per weight:
  - Under 15 pounds
  - 15 pounds and under 20 pounds
  - 20 pounds and not to exceed 25 pounds.

- The Boston Terrier must display a striking square appearance through a balance of length and the length of the dog's body.

- It should not appear either coarse or spindly but it must be seen as a sturdy little dog.

- Its muscle and bone must be well proportioned, especially through its dog's weight and structure.

- Fault
  - chunky or blocky in appearance.
  - Influence of Sex.
    - There is a slight refinement for the female's conformation, but the rest are the same.

Head:

- The dog's skull is flat on top, square, flat cheeks, free from any wrinkles, brow abrupt and the stop well defined.
- The expression of an ideal Boston Terrier is kind and alert, which will indicate a high degree of intelligent. This is one of the most import characteristic of the Boston Terrier breed.
- The eyes are large, wide apart, and dark in color, and round.
- The Boston Terrier's eyes are set square in their skull and the outside corners of their eyes are on line with their cheeks when you view them from the front.
- Disqualify
  - The color of the eyes is blue or if there are any traces of blue.

- The Boston Terrier's ears are carried erect, small, either cropped or natural to conform to the head's shape or near the corner of the skulls.
- Your Boston Terrier's muzzle is wide, short, square, and deep and in proportion to the skull.
- The muzzle is short, square, wide and deep and in proportion to the skull.
- The muzzle must be free from any wrinkles.
- It must be shorter in length than in depth or width, but not exceeding the length, or one-third of the length of the skull.
- The muzzle must be parallel from the top of the skull.
- The dog's nose must be wide and black, with a clear definition of a line between the nostrils.
- Disqualify
  - Dudley nose
- The dog's jaw must be square and broad with short but still regular teeth.
- The dog's bite is sufficiently undershot to the muzzle or is pretty even.
- The Boston Terrier displays a good depth of chops, but not really pendulous, and must cover the teeth when the mouth is fully closed.
- Serious Fault
  - Wry mouth.
- Head Faults
- The eyes are displaying too much haw or too white.

- The nostrils are wide or pinched.
- Ear size is not really proportionate to the head.
- If there is a showing of teeth or tongue when the dog's mouth is closed.

Neck, Topline and Body:

- The length of the Boston Terrier's neck should display an image of balance of the whole feature of the dog.
- It must be slightly arched, which is carried gracefully, and setting very neatly on the dog' shoulder.
- The dog's back must be short enough to squarely frame the dog's body.
- The dog's topline must be level.
- The rump curves slightly on the set-on of the dog's tail.
- The dog's chest should be deep with a good with.
- Its ribs must be well sprung and carried very well on the back to the loins.
- The Boston Terrier's body should appear short.
- Its tail should be set on low, fine and tapering, short, screw or straight, and should not be carried above horizontal.
- Disqualify
  - Docked tail.
  - Gaily carried tail.
  - Roach back

- ◦ sway back
- ◦ slab - sided.

Forequarters

- The shoulders should be well laid back and sloping, which gives the Boston Terrier a vision of finesse when walking.
- The elbows stand neither out nor in.
- The forelegs should be wide apart but still on a line with the tip of the shoulder blade.
- The forelegs should be straight in bone with strong, short pasterns.
- The dewclaws could be removed.
- The feet are round, neither in nor out, small, with well arched toes and short nails.
- Faults
  - ◦ Legs lacking in substance
  - ◦ play feet.

Hindquarters:

- The thighs should be well muscled and strong, bent at the stifles and be set true.
- The hocks should be short to the feet, not in or out, but with well - defined hock joint.
- The feet must be compact and small with short nails.
- Fault
  - ◦ Straight in stifle.

Gait:

- The gait of a Boston Terrier should be laid straight ahead, in line with perfect rhythm, and each step of the dog should indicate power and grace.
- Gait Faults
  - There will be no rolling, paddling, or weaving, when gaited.
  - Hackney gait.
  - Any crossing movement, either front or rear.

Coat:

- short,
- smooth
- bright
- fine in texture.

Color and Markings:

- Brindle, seal, or black with white markings.
- Brindle is preferred over all the other markings available for the Boston Terrier
- Disqualify
  - Solid black
  - solid brindle
  - solid seal without required white markings.
  - Any color not described in the standard.
- Required Markings

- White muzzle band, white blaze between the eyes, white forechest.

- Desired Markings:
  - White muzzle band, even white blaze between the eyes and over the head, white collar, white forechest, white on part or whole of forelegs and hind legs below the hocks.
  - A dog with a preponderance of white on the head or body must possess sufficient merit otherwise to counteract its deficiencies.

Temperament:
- friendly
- lively dog.
- The breed has an excellent disposition and a high degree of intelligence, which makes the Boston Terrier an incomparable companion.

The dog must be clean-cut, coupled with unique characteristics based on the breed standards. It should result to a charming and dapper, true gentleman, Boston Terrier.

Scale of Points

General Appearance	10
Expression	10
Head (Muzzle, Jaw, Bite, Skull & Stop)	15
Eyes	5
Ears	5
Neck, Topline, Body & Tail	15
Forequarters	10
Hindquarters	10
Feet	5
Color, Coat & Markings	5
Gait	10
Total	100

These are just some of the things that you need to know if you want to show off your Boston Terrier. Make sure you prepare the dog for the big day and make sure that you are well-prepared. Do not go into shows unless you know what you are doing.

Boston Terrier Care Sheet

We have traveled a lot to get through this point! Are you glad you have finished the journey in the world of Boston Terriers? This breed will surely love you and be with your side willing to cuddle and play with you. It is now time to go out and buy your very first dog.

We have already discussed a lot of things about this breed, starting from its wonderful history, breeding guidelines, and even food amounts. Make sure you use this knowledge on your pet.

Boston Terrier 101

Origin: United States

Pedigree: cross breed of the English Bulldog and the English Terrier (which is now extinct)

Breed Size: non-sporting group

Body Type and Appearance: smooth coated, short-headed, built compactly, short-tailed, but still well balanced.

Group: American Kennel Club

Height: Males are 17 inches tall and Females stand at 16 inches tall.

Weight: 15-25 lbs. for males while 10-20 lbs. for females

Coat Length: short and flat

Coat Texture: glossy

Color: brindle with white, black and white, seal with white

Temperament: friendly, lively, intelligent,

Strangers: friendly around strangers

Other Dogs: loves other dogs

Other Pets: gets along well with other pets

Training: easy to train

Exercise Needs: less than 20 to 40 minutes of exercise per day

Health Conditions: overall healthy but may come across several diseases or illnesses due to their brachycephalic (squashed face)

Lifespan: average 10-14 years

Home Requirements

Recommended Accessories: harness, dog bed, food/water dishes, grooming supplies crate, toys, collar, leash

 Collar and Harness: sized by weight

Grooming Supplies: few kinds of brushes nail trimmers, and fluffy towels

Grooming Frequency: weekly brushing and monthly bathing and nail trimming

Energy Level: alert little creatures that will certainly get its way

Exercise Requirements: they do not really need a lot of exercise

Crate: you can use this as a mode of transportation

Crate Size: small to medium

Food/Water Bowl: Depend you and your lifestyle, but make sure that the one you choose will last a life time.

Toys: give enough toys to feed its curious mind.

Training: easy to train, loves human companion

Nutritional Needs

Nutritional Needs: water, vitamins, minerals, carbohydrate, protein, fats

 Calorie Needs: enough calories is only needed as they may get fat easily

Amount to Feed (puppy): you can do trial and error method, or even consult your vet for the proper feeding guide

Amount to Feed (adult): change food amount base on activity and weight

Important Ingredients: fresh animal protein (chicken, turkey, beef, lamb, eggs), digestible carbohydrates (rice, oats, barley), animal fats

Important Minerals: calcium, magnesium, manganese phosphorus, potassium iron, copper

Important Vitamins: Vitamin D, Vitamin A, Vitamin B-12, Vitamin C

Glossary of Dog Terms

Abundism – Referring to a pup that has markings more prolific than is normal.

Acariasis – A type of mite infection.

ACF – Australian Pup Federation

Affix – A puptery name that follows the pup's registered name; puptery owner, not the breeder of the pup.

Agouti – A type of natural coloring pattern in which individual hairs have bands of light and dark coloring.

Ailurophile – A person who loves pups.

Albino – A type of genetic mutation which results in little to no pigmentation, in the eyes, skin, and coat.

Allbreed – Referring to a show that accepts all breeds or a judge who is qualified to judge all breeds.

Alley Pup – A non-pedigreed pup.

Alter – A desexed pup; a male pup that has been neutered or a female that has been spayed.

Amino Acid – The building blocks of protein; there are 22 types for pups, 11 of which can be synthesized and 11 which must come from the diet (see essential amino acid).

Anestrus – The period between estrus cycles in a female pup.

Any Other Variety (AOV) – A registered pup that doesn't conform to the breed standard.

ASH – American Shorthair, a breed of pup.

Back Cross – A type of breeding in which the offspring is mated back to the parent.

Balance – Referring to the pup's structure; proportional in accordance with the breed standard.

Barring – Describing the tabby's striped markings.

Base Color – The color of the coat.

Bicolor – A pup with patched color and white.

Blaze – A white coloring on the face, usually in the shape of an inverted V.

Bloodline – The pedigree of the pup.

Brindle – A type of coloring, a brownish or tawny coat with streaks of another color.

Castration – The surgical removal of a male pup's testicles.

Pup Show – An event where pups are shown and judged.

Puptery – A registered pup breeder; also, a place where pups may be boarded.

CFA – The Pup Fanciers Association.

Cobby – A compact body type.

Colony – A group of pups living wild outside.

Color Point – A type of coat pattern that is controlled by color point alleles; pigmentation on the tail, legs, face, and ears with an ivory or white coat.

Colostrum – The first milk produced by a lactating female; contains vital nutrients and antibodies.

Conformation – The degree to which a pedigreed pup adheres to the breed standard.

Cross Breed – The offspring produced by mating two distinct breeds.

Dam – The female parent.

Declawing – The surgical removal of the pup's claw and first toe joint.

Developed Breed – A breed that was developed through selective breeding and crossing with established breeds.

Down Hairs – The short, fine hairs closest to the body which keep the pup warm.

DSH – Domestic Shorthair.

Estrus – The reproductive cycle in female pups during which she becomes fertile and receptive to mating.

Fading Pup Syndrome – Pups that die within the first two weeks after birth; the cause is generally unknown.

Feral – A wild, untamed pup of domestic descent.

Gestation – Pregnancy; the period during which the fetuses develop in the female's uterus.

Guard Hairs – Coarse, outer hairs on the coat.

Harlequin – A type of coloring in which there are van markings of any color with the addition of small patches of the same color on the legs and body.

Inbreeding – The breeding of related pups within a closed group or breed.

Kibble – Another name for dry pup food.

Lilac – A type of coat color that is pale pinkish-gray.

Line – The pedigree of ancestors; family tree.

Litter – The name given to a group of pups born at the same time from a single female.

Mask – A type of coloring seen on the face in some breeds.

Matts – Knots or tangles in the pup's fur.

Mittens – White markings on the feet of a pup.

Moggie – Another name for a mixed breed pup.

Mutation – A change in the DNA of a cell.

Muzzle – The nose and jaws of an animal.

Natural Breed – A breed that developed without selective breeding or the assistance of humans.

Neutering – Desexing a male pup.

Open Show – A show in which spectators are allowed to view the judging.

Pads – The thick skin on the bottom of the feet.

Particolor – A type of coloration in which there are markings of two or more distinct colors.

Patched – A type of coloration in which there is any solid color, tabby, or tortoiseshell color plus white.

Pedigree – A purebred pup; the pup's papers showing its family history.

Pet Quality – A pup that is not deemed of high enough standard to be shown or bred.

Piebald – A pup with white patches of fur.

Points – Also color points; markings of contrasting color on the face, ears, legs, and tail.

Pricked – Referring to ears that sit upright.

Purebred – A pedigreed pup.

Queen – An intact female pup.

Roman Nose – A type of nose shape with a bump or arch.

Scruff – The loose skin on the back of a pup's neck.

Selective Breeding – A method of modifying or improving a breed by choosing pups with desirable traits.

Senior – A pup that is more than 5 but less than 7 years old.

Sire – The male parent of a pup.

Solid – Also self; a pup with a single coat color.

Spay – Desexing a female pup.

Stud – An intact male pup.

Tabby – A type of coat pattern consisting of a contrasting color over a ground color.

Tom Pup – An intact male pup.

Tortoiseshell – A type of coat pattern consisting of a mosaic of red or cream and another base color.

Tri-Color – A type of coat pattern consisting of three distinct colors in the coat.

Tuxedo – A black and white pup.

Unaltered – A pup that has not been desexed.

Index

M

N

O

P

S

T

Photo Credits

Page Photo by user Mike Lavoie via Flickr.com,

https://www.flickr.com/photos/cpc-a-gogo/2455916360/

Page Photo by user lezumbalaberenjena via Flickr.com,

https://www.flickr.com/photos/14020964@N02/11242155964/

Page Photo by user Nick via Flickr.com,

https://www.flickr.com/photos/25423804@N03/2959535523/

Page Photo by user Sendai Blog via Flickr.com,

https://www.flickr.com/photos/sendaiblog/7615314820/

Page Photo by user Sendai Blog via Flickr.com,

https://www.flickr.com/photos/sendaiblog/4863524650/

Page Photo by user Sendai Blog via Flickr.com,

https://www.flickr.com/photos/sendaiblog/4863523410/

Page Photo by user david takes photos via Flickr.com,

https://www.flickr.com/photos/dcaloren/3969481282/

Page Photo by user Stephy 7 via Flickr.com,

https://www.flickr.com/photos/59306869@N03/5435561142/

References

"Boston Terrier: The American Gentleman… Who Farts a Lot" – TerriblyTerrier.com

https://terriblyterrier.com/boston-terrier/

"Boston Terrier - History and Health" – PetWave.com

https://www.petwave.com/Dogs/Breeds/Boston-Terrier/Overview.aspx

"Boston Terrier Dog Breed Information and Personality Traits" – Hillspet.com

https://www.hillspet.com/dog-care/dog-breeds/boston-terrier

"Boston Terrier Temperament: What's Good About 'Em, What's Bad About 'Em" – YourPureBredPuppy.com

http://www.yourpurebredpuppy.com/reviews/bostonterriers.html

"Boston Terrier" – PetGuide.com

https://www.petguide.com/breeds/dog/boston-terrier

"Looking for a Boston Terrier" – Pets4Homes.co.uk

https://www.pets4homes.co.uk/dog-breeds/boston-terrier/

"Boston Terrier" – EasyPetMD.com

http://www.easypetmd.com/doginfo/boston-terrier

"Boston Terrier" – Vetwest.com.au

https://www.vetwest.com.au/pet-library/boston-terrier

"Boston Terrier" – Purina.com

https://www.purina.com/dogs/dog-breeds/boston-terrier

"Boston Terrier" – Bterrier.com

http://www.bterrier.com

"Boston Terrier Official Breed Standard" – AKC.org

https://images.akc.org/pdf/breeds/standards/BostonTerrier.pdf

"Boston Terrier" – AKC.org

https://www.akc.org/dog-breeds/boston-terrier/

Feeding Baby

Newborn to 24 Months

Including breast feeding, baby
formula, store bought vs.
homemade baby food, recipes,
equipment, kitchenware, natural
food, organic food, charts,
scheduling, and much more!

Cynthia Cherry

Feeding Baby
Cynthia Cherry
978-1941070000

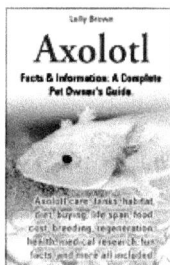

Lolly Brown

Axolotl

Facts & Information: A Complete
Pet Owner's Guide.

Axolotl care, tanks, habitat,
diet, buying, life span, food,
cost, breeding, regeneration,
health, medical research, fun
facts, and more all included!

Axolotl
Lolly Brown
978-0989658430

Dysautonomia,
POTS Syndrome

Facts &
Information

Diagnosis, symptoms, treatment, causes, doctors,
nervous disorders, prognosis, research, history,
diet, physical therapy, medication, environment,
and more all covered!

Frederick Earlstein

Dysautonomia, POTS
Syndrome
Frederick Earlstein
978-0989658485

Degenerative
Disc Disease
Explained

Facts & Information

Including treatment,
surgery, symptoms,
exercises, causes,
physical therapy,
neck, back pain, and
much more!

Frederick Earlstein

Degenerative Disc
Disease Explained
Frederick Earlstein
978-0989658485

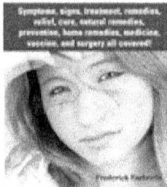

Sinusitis, Hay Fever,
Allergic Rhinitis Explained
Frederick Earlstein
978-1941070024

Wicca
Riley Star
978-1941070130

Zombie Apocalypse
Rex Cutty
978-1941070154

Capybara
Lolly Brown
978-1941070062

Eels As Pets
Lolly Brown
978-1941070167

Scabies and Lice Explained
Frederick Earlstein
978-1941070017

Saltwater Fish As Pets
Lolly Brown
978-0989658461

Torticollis Explained
Frederick Earlstein
978-1941070055

Kennel Cough
Lolly Brown
978-0989658409

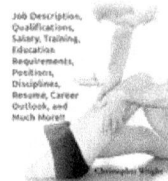

Physiotherapist, Physical
Therapist
Christopher Wright
978-0989658492

Rats, Mice, and Dormice
As Pets
Lolly Brown
978-1941070079

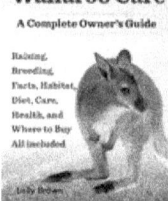

Wallaby and Wallaroo Care
Lolly Brown
978-1941070031

Bodybuilding Supplements
Explained
Jon Shelton
978-1941070239

Demonology
Riley Star
978-19401070314

Pigeon Racing
Lolly Brown
978-1941070307

Dwarf Hamster
Lolly Brown
978-1941070390

Cryptozoology
Rex Cutty
978-1941070406

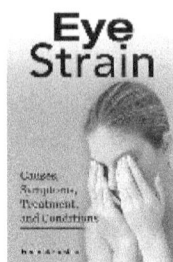

Eye Strain
Frederick Earlstein
978-1941070369

Inez The Miniature Elephant
Asher Ray
978-1941070353

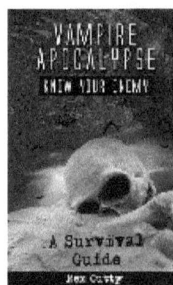

Vampire Apocalypse
Rex Cutty
978-1941070321

www.ingramcontent.com/pod-product-compliance
Lightning Source LLC
LaVergne TN
LVHW051644080426
835511LV00016B/2476